PUBLISHED by PARABLES
*Earthly Stories with a Heavenly Meaning*

# Imparting Of The Moral Values To Others
# By
# Orex Kombea

PUBLISHED by PARABLES
*Earthly Stories with a Heavenly Meaning*

Imparting Of The Moral Values To Others
By Orex Kombea

Published By Parables
May, 2021

All Rights Reserved. No part of this book may be reproduced or utilized in any form or by any means, electronic or mechanical, including photocopying, **recording, or by any information storage and retrieval system, without permission in writing from the author.**

Printed in the United States of America

Readers should be aware that Internet Web sites offered as citations and/or sources for further information may have been changed or disappeared between the time this was written and the time it is read.

# Imparting Of The Moral Values To Others
# By
# Orex Kombea

# FORWARD

Every person is unique and outstanding. That means the way of life each person lives is different to each other. The physical appearance like built is not the same to each other. The look of the facial views are not the same to each other. Therefore, we can say that there is you and you alone. You are not two or three. I am I alone. I am not two or three. There is no any you anywhere. There is no any me anywhere. Therefore, there is never and never for two beings for one person.

The characters and the traits as human being is differ since each is individual. Each person's ways are his/her ways. No matter what race each belong to, what gender each is, what age group each is, how old each is, what value each has, what category each places, what physical appearance each has, what family each is derived and belong to, and list goes on.

There are common emphasis and ethical values that every person have as human being is automatically impacted for living. The life about the social valued concepts are to bound by everyone. The common cultural areas where a person practices and lives as life are; using of regional or national language, access to education, understand sports codes and rules to perform, usage of currency for buying goods and services, practice religious activities and ideologies, making dressing according each gender, access to health services, the constitutional regulations to abide for, and many more.

      Nevertheless, every human being is meant to reproduce, eat and live, sheltered in house, cloth to keep warm and cover shame, protect one and other, raise youngs, cater food, conserve environment, breed animals, setting up settlements, forming organizations, operate and regulate business, causing massive destructions in the natural environments like mining and logging, making inventions of machinery equipments, educative, performing ritual activities, and more and more others.
The ethical moral life is inbuilt that lives by mankind on Earth which seems common. But it depends on how individuals that utilize it. Performing or putting out the best moral values and good qualities to others and the surrounding is the uniqueness, positive outcome so that it is the way known an outshining of the best personalities.

On the other hand, the negative or opposite side is where immoral ways of life that lives by mankind. Not every individual is morally perfect. That means every person makes mistake by living unrighteous or immoral in their deeds towards others or to their surroundings or even to themselves. Sometimes some people choose to live the immoral lives. Their characters and behaviors towards others and their environment is done or performed in unacceptable behavior and manner. That kind of live is bad and unacceptable which has resulted for problematic consequences. The example of immorality lives are mostly the common crimes and the others similar; fight, murder, swear, robe, steal, gossip, disobeying, blasphemy, dishonesty, lie, deceiving, misleading, mistreatment, murdering, thief, ignorance, rape, stigmatization, adultery, discrimination, teasing, bullying, prostitution, cruelness, backbiting, neglecting, fornication, gambling, taking illicit drugs, looting, argument, and more to name.

As human being everyone is always trying to live morally. Moral law is inbuilt in human heart and conscious human element so that every person grows with it. Guidance and mentoring from the parents to child is where he or she starts to pick up and to learn, and understands fully and confirms the morality. The ethical values being thought are good for personal moral. From there he or she starts to live the valuable life. So what is good and what is bad is what to determine.

Now, into this approach you will be guided and be given some insight knowledge and concept thoughts about the good quality deeds that have to be put or be imparted into others' lives. The good behavioral deeds are the positive moral values in actual actions which are acceptable and relevant characters.

The examples of positive and moral values, and distinctive principles; share, smile, greet, love, pity, mercy, grace, care, assist, kindness, generous, obey, respect, help, honest, humility, fairness, faithfulness, calm, peace, joy, loyal, harmony, candid, treat, mentoring, submit, gentleness, frank, and more. The applying of the above moral values to others and the surrounding is; 'sharing is caring, giving is blessing' which becomes the outshining the inner personalities.

To share and give things to others is broad meaning and considerable. We do share or do give out belongings, properties or offers to others within or without relationship. That is sharing and caring. There in many areas we do share and care which becomes blessing to us and to receivers. For these reasons we will look at distinguished areas that we will share to care for the others and the reasonable persons and the nature.

# Contents

GIVING TO GOD ALMIGHTY ............................................................... 1
GIVING TO GOD'S SERVANT ............................................................... 4
GIVING TO THE SICK PATIENT ........................................................... 7
GIVING TO THE INMATE .................................................................... 10
GIVING TO THE POOR ....................................................................... 12
GIVING TO THE HANDICAPPED ........................................................ 16
GIVING TO THE OLD PERSON ........................................................... 20
GIVING TO THE WIDOW .................................................................... 23
GIVING TO THE STRANGER ............................................................... 26
GIVING TO THE NEIGHBOR ............................................................... 28
GIVING TO THE VISITOR ................................................................... 30
GIVING TO THE ORPHAN .................................................................. 33
GIVING TO THE WIDOWER ............................................................... 36
GIVING TO THE PARENTS ................................................................. 39
GIVING TO THE STUDENT ................................................................. 42
GIVING TO THE COMMUNITY .......................................................... 45
GIVING TO THE ADOPTED CHILD .................................................... 48
GIVING TO A PET ............................................................................... 51
GIVING TO THE LEADER ................................................................... 54
GIVING TO THE SERVANT ................................................................. 56
GIVING TO THE FOREIGNER ............................................................. 59
GIVING TO THE DOMESTIC ANIMALS ............................................. 61
GIVING TO THE HOMELESS .............................................................. 63
GIVING TO THE JOBLESS ................................................................... 66
GIVING TO THE ASYLUM SEEKERS .................................................. 69
GIVING TO THE SUPERIOR ................................................................ 72
GIVING TO THE COMMON LAW BREAKERS ................................... 75
GIVING TO THE CHURCH .................................................................. 78
GIVING TO THE CHILD ...................................................................... 80
GIVING TO THE DISASTER VICTIMS ................................................ 82
GIVING TO THE ELDERLY PEOPLE ................................................... 85
GIVING TO THE INTERRACIAL ......................................................... 88
GIVING TO THE WEALTHY PERSON ................................................. 90
GIVING TO THE LIER AND CON PERSON ........................................ 93
GIVING TO THE ENVIRONMENT ...................................................... 96
THE SUMMARY ................................................................................... 98

# IMPARTING OF THE MORAL VALUES
## SHARING IS CARING, GIVING IS BLESSING THAT OUTSHINES INNER PERSONALITIES:

## *GIVING TO GOD ALMIGHTY*

Giving to God almighty is many in focus. But into this context we will look at few. How will we give to God, and what is that be? When will we give to God? Why will we give to God? These are some of the questionnaires that we might consider ourselves. Apart from all other giving, importantly God only wants a person's life. God deserves righteous and the holy life. To qualify for that standard there are multiples of ritual activities that we might perform.

It is natural that every mankind has to die. Every man borns to die. While waiting for die there are some purposeful duties and work everyone has to perform. The way and the character of God is holy and righteous. Every human being has to follow God's way of life and meet the standard requirements which is holiness. Every mankind is God's image, and God does not want anyone to loose.

## Orex Kombea

God loves every single person but hates inequities that mankind performs. That is why most people will lose.

There are also other ritual activities which are noble as supporting the work of God. It is by proclaiming his message, witness the others about good news, support the church or religious activities, participate and take part, teach or educate about his love and grace, reach out and proclaim the message, encourage others in righteous life and live holy. Preach or share the word of God to others. And there are many things we can do to boost the word of God. These are some of the criteria that we will meet, and become faultless and fullness in God's sights. Human being is worshipping creature from God's purpose. Since then he/she has to worship God with full strength, with whole heart, and with whole mind. Praise and worship songs are to be sang frequently in fullness through the fellowship in sole or combine is the focal purpose. Watch and pray often which is the strength that enables the faith's firmness. The performing of these ritual activities are to become life for those whom are called for. That is where he/she gives his/her life in the best on his/her abilities to perform in God's service.

## IMPARTING OF THE MORAL VALUES
Therefore, sharing is caring, and giving is blessing that let your inner personalities outshine.

Orex Kombea

## *GIVING TO GOD'S SERVANT*

God's servant is a God representer. God will not physically present as human being and perform his mission or work by himself. Therefore there has to be someone who will represent him. Every human being is godlike since he/she is God's image and yet a small god.

God's mission is a noble work that only few people chooses to do from the most rest others. There are so many people who know the good about the message and the mission of God but they don't want to be the part takers. They even do not want to obey. Rather, they live their own way of life which is ungodly. Religious work is a voluntary work and someone has become volunteer to perform.

The world is offering the countless attractive lives. Wherefore people's concentrations are focused on them and be kept on them. The works of the worldly world are broad and diverse to number. They are both good and evil. That is where

## IMPARTING OF THE MORAL VALUES

more and more people are diverting their causes and interests on them. Those types of people in most and are spiritually blind. There is someone who stands up, saying I will do the work. That is to be a real person who wants to be the servant of God. Start preparing himself/herself in some extents. For that idea there are some people who stand up to carry it is as career. Those types particulars are especially priests, bishops, pastors, saints, apostles, ministers, teachers, preachers, proclaimers and so on. That is where they share to care which seems giving is blessing.

To do the work of God is not that simple and easy. If someone like the above figures want to impart the word of God to people, and perform the religious mission activities related are so difficult and challenging. But somehow with the help of God's power people tend to be religious from the witness and the performances of those religious figures. In most, the rebirths are compromised and organize the gathering places as the church grounds. They build synagogues or shelters for worship and buildings.

Orex Kombea

As the member of religion community and the religious being he/she might do some things worth and good for those figures. That is through supporting them by providing the rare needs in terms of food, cloth, money, shelter, and others accordingly and whichever appreciate with giving heart and full moral. Sharing is caring.

To support the servant is not only the ones whom you know by person or the ones you always support. But you can give support whichever way to the servants that seems strange to you. That means you can support street preacher, and whoever performs for the gospel's sake. If you share and care for such people like them then giving becomes blessing that outshines your inner personalities.

# IMPARTING OF THE MORAL VALUES

## *GIVING TO THE SICK PATIENT*

We all feel sick or have sick and experience what all being like patient is. Sometimes sick can be in serious condition, sometimes it can be in less serious. That is where we need someone who can always be close with us that will comfort us and cure the sick. Else we do some things to heal. Also we need help and hoping that I might be well and back to normalcy soon. Some sicknesses that we have might be chronic and long-term suffering.

The treatment location for sick is clinic. The health workers whom dealt with the sick patients are there to help. How do you feel when your doctor or nurse treat you with comfort? What do you feel when you are dosed with the prescribed pills from your doctor or nurse? What do you feel when someone religious like pastor visit you and prays for you on your sick bad? What do you feel when someone special in the community or the society like member of parliament visit you when you are in your sick bad? How do you feel when someone who is a member of your family or relative visit you with comfort? What do you feel when someone who is poor in the community but really concerns for you and visit you? What do you feel when someone who is rich in a community or a society where you live visit you on your sick bed? What do you feel when some people your friends or workmates or playmates or church members visit you? What do you feel when someone less fortunate as the common named people like culprits or prostitutes visit you when you are in your sick bed? What do you feel when a handicapped person visit you when you are in your sick bed? What do you feel when someone too old whom you know visit you when you are in your sick bed? Or what do you feel if someone you do not know you visit you? These are some of the situational questions. The answer to these questions will be; you will give all your heart to them. You will think these people are the really concerned ones for me. Your mind will work out, what will I do to these people if I get back to normal? You will feel that these are very concerning people to me, and you will try to value them in many ways as you be pleased. Even you will weep with the shedding tears.

## IMPARTING OF THE MORAL VALUES

Treating or giving to someone who is sick with kind or essential is really a blessing. If you want to give something to such people then give them with sincerely heart. Do not expect something in return. Even do not let anyone or your neighbor see that you will gain approval. Also do not give in public so that you will be praised. Giving to a sick people we must gave with compassionate heart. Not only giving but assist him/her in whichever the condition and the situation the sick person faces. Therefore, sharing is caring, and giving is blessing that let your inner personalities outshine.

Orex Kombea

## *GIVING TO THE INMATE*

How will the inmates/prisoners be given what we want to give? Why do they detain? What makes them imprisoned? In common sense we quickly assume that the prisoner is the law breaker. The justice has its jurisdictions to prove whether a particular person is guilty or not. We will not condone the guilty and convictions he/she commits. The prisoner faces consequences which he/she deserves.

There is none righteous. Not even single. Everyone makes mistake. But inmates are the ones that break constructional laws witnessed by someone authorized person or any body else. So, how will you visit and make kind to them since they are behind the bars for good deeds? Why will the custodians let people visit the prisoner? Sometimes prisoner be your relative or someone your friend or the one that you know well like friend to you. Well, there are certain times that the custodians allow the family members and the relatives visit them as scheduled according human rights law. From there you can visit them if you have heart for him/her then.

## IMPARTING OF THE MORAL VALUES

The detainee is similar as sick or helpless person. He/She desperately needs someone's visit. His/Her heart be with you when you visit to do kind.

There are many people who have love and pity for the detainees but how will they visit them since detain zone is not a free general public area. On the other hand they are fully corrected by law. Also the religious people relief them from worries and afflictions.

Ways of offering prayer is only option to those who have good heart which don't visit physically for the detainees. It is not the actual action that approval has to gain. It is a spiritual connection so that prayer will reach to the detainee for blessings, comfort and guidance. Therefore, sharing is caring, and giving is blessing that let your inner personalities outshine.

Orex Kombea

## *GIVING TO THE POOR*

We regard the people those with no possessions or have little is poor. They are inadequate and have insufficient to live. That is where their living is different. Poor can be in individual, sometimes can be in family or in more families or in a whole community.

In fact people are not meant to be poor. There are some factors that cause people poor. What are some of the factors that cause poor? They are like the geographical landscape which is not suitable that they might cultivate, they have no customary land that they might sustain gardening, their state owns every landmass, their state runs every business operations, their government does not create sufficient job employment opportunities, overcrowded population in an area, evicted from the disaster, migrate from the social unrest, migrate from the war.

Sometimes people become poor because of the physical disabilities. Sometimes people become poor because of the laziness which they always expecting from someone or having free

## IMPARTING OF THE MORAL VALUES

handouts. Sometimes people are heavily depend on others. Most of all the poor people are cognitively uncreative. Creativity costs nothing as the saying goes. For this reason almost global population lives a productive and creative lives.

How can you tell or class someone who is poor? There are many areas that you can workout for the proves. They will be examined through the types of clothes that they wear which is cheaper, they wear same old clothes for prolong, they wear torned and unfit most often, their bodies seem unclean and rough for quite long period of time.

They don't live in the decent homes. They are homeless. They live under the city shelters or under the bridges. They don't eat good balanced diets. They eat garbage foods. Their family members be in the similar look some times. They sometimes beg in the streets.

How may you give or provide for the poor? It is easy. Just give him or her anything that you wish. You will not be selective in items that you will give. The poor will always appreciate to whatever that you give. Sometimes you are not prepared and suddenly you meet the poor person in your way. In that case you may greet him or just offer him/her with whatever item or money that you have in right. You must always give with sincere heart. If not you may pass on.

Sometimes it has to be given or donated to the mass poor population. By then you will have to provide towards the contribution. From there you must give the best in whatever measures they have to be. Do not give unnecessary or valueless items. Always give the best to poor unless you do not have that value. Giving to poor in whichever way is one of the positive way of life. Therefore you must give to the poor with love and compassion.

How does poor feel whenever he/she receives items from someone? Just imagine, as a human being he/she feels so pleased and happy. The poor person has to appreciate you with loving and kind heart. Sometimes that person perform actions in some gestures while receiving items. That is the manifestation of appreciation. Other times they will say good words like 'thankyou'.

## IMPARTING OF THE MORAL VALUES

Sometimes someone gives items to poor in the eyes of many maybe the right idea. By doing that, the giver is showing example to others. But, into other view it is not good way to give in the eyes of many. Rather, give when there is no body watching. Even do not snap with your camera while giving to poor. Therefore, sharing is caring, and giving is blessing that let your inner personalities outshine.

Orex Kombea

## *GIVING TO THE HANDICAPPED*

What is handicap? It is disadvantage of a particular person with physical disabilities. There are some people who are handicapped in the communities that where we live. Sometimes the handicapped person can be one of the family members or a relative. It could be a neighbor as well.

When examining all body parts each has distinguished functions that performs the meaningful purposes for the whole entire body. The functions and purposes that perform or serve by the eyes for the whole body cannot be done by the ears. The functions and purposes that perform or serve by the legs for the whole body cannot be done by the arms. The functions and purposes that performs or serves by stomach for the whole body cannot be done by the head. And similar ideas go on for the rest of the body parts.

Those types of people are in some sorts of special needs. Mostly in some areas are better for such people like them because their government provides them with special need equipments and

## IMPARTING OF THE MORAL VALUES

facilities so that they can access the easy life. For example; a cripple with wheel chair, and an ear impairment with hearing aid. On the other hand their government provides most essential services like education and health and set rights.

In some areas the equal distribution of government aids is not effective or not functioning properly. However, some are not access to the government services or they locate to the isolations because on the developmental status of their country.

As an individual, how do you examine or consider the handicapped person when it comes in your view? What do you do when you see him/her? What do you feel when you see someone with disabilities? In fact, for my case I feel pity on him/her. Sometimes in most I do give the things that available in my hand like food or money but in secret which other people may not notice.

All of us as human beings there are some things that we will do to those handicapped people. None other than giving is a particular area in sharing for caring. You just give to such people whichever way and whatever you have. You must give with compensate heart with love and care. Or you must feed him/her as you wish. Take him/her has you take yourself since you both are human bounds. Talk good and kindly to them whichever way you wish.

There are some testimonial occasions which I see in one of the countries in African Continent. There is someone who is a well known godly man by the name of Prophet T.B Joshua. In most times he gather all the handicaps together in a synagogue and present them with surplus of food rations, money in thousands, and aids in quantities the wheel chairs. He also pays tuition fees for the student group. In another occasion he also bought a brand new car for a crippled Masters program student in Business Economics at Abia State University.

There was something good impressive happened when receiving the gifts. They feel happy and pleased. Many of them burst in tears of joy.

We do not know the thoughts and the feelings of the handicapped people. Maybe they wish to be like the able people to achieve some goals and meet some standards in life. But that will

## IMPARTING OF THE MORAL VALUES

not eventuate in their lives. Therefore they need some aid and help in some measures so give to them in whichever way you think will meet his/her needs. For that case just give and help with whichever way you afford will benefit him/her. Therefore, sharing is caring and giving is blessing that let your inner personalities outshines.

Orex Kombea

## *GIVING TO THE OLD PERSON*

Old person is someone could be the least privileged. The stage of old person is when someone who moves around with moving aid, like walking stick and wheelchair. The strength of old person is declining as he/she grows old. That means some of his/her body system are not functioning properly or completely out of function. In most cases the systems of the body easily declining of functioning the normal way. For example; eyes start getting blind or completely bind, ears start getting deaf or completely deaf, teeth start getting loose or completely loose. And the similar happenings take place in all other parts of the body systems.

Old person always be the father/ mother of someone or grandparents or relative to someone. He/She is under care in some measures from the relatives or children or grandchildren. He/She is treated differently from others according his/her needs. This type of care and guide is mostly practiced in the underdeveloped and developing countries. In developed countries, mostly the old

## IMPARTING OF THE MORAL VALUES

people are under the custody of government. Which means every old person is cared by his/her government in all measures.

As an individual, how do you share to care for old people? There are more different approaches. The old person can be your father/mother. It can be your grand father/mother. Sometimes be your grand father/mother. On the other means can be your relative or someone in your community.

There are different areas when you come to approach the old person. The 'sharing is caring' for old person are in these areas. Do not abuse him/her by swearing, negatively criticizing, condemning, teasing, discriminating, stigmatizing, neglecting, deceiving, and applying of more other inappropriate attitudes.

There are inverse attitudes from above stated areas that we look in to offer for the old person in the notion in 'sharing is caring' and 'giving is bleeding'. Do kind actions; by taking care, by loving, by helping and assisting, by offering the worthy and valuable objects, by feeding, and the rest other positive deeds when it comes to your approach. That is where as human being the old person heart is none other but you alone. For those cases the old person is

## Orex Kombea

someone who is the first to see the rising and setting of sun, and faced the world with the worldly experiences unlike you. Therefore, sharing is caring, and giving is blessing that let your inner personalities outshine.

# IMPARTING OF THE MORAL VALUES

## *GIVING TO THE WIDOW*

Who is widow? How do you give to widow? When do you give to widow, and why? Widow is someone who is her husband already passed/died. She could be in her young age with unweaned younger children. She could be an old lady with grown-up children. Other could be a widow with no children which is a single lady.

Matter of fact most windows are the ones that face the life being without husband in various measures in certain. That means the lives being widow to a wife is different. There are many areas in which life has to go through by doubling up areas both for father and mother. Windows with children are the ones that really face the challenging family life. The lives that face by being widow compared to being wife is different. She lives the different life altogether which is tougher and challenging for the good's sake.

From the absence of the presence of father as the family head a window mother with unweaned children is very challenging. She has to carry out both the father's and mother's tasks. For instance; if she has to build a house then she builds, if she has to make fence then she makes, if she has to provide food for the household then she provides, if she has to provide tuition fees for her children then she provides, if she has to make garden then she makes, If she has to contribute towards the community or society then she contributes. She has to carry out every role and responsibility that both father and mother perform. Since then, she is both the father and the mother at the same time for the children, and the community, or the society that whichever way or however she performs.

There are ways in which you do when it comes to your approach the window in your community or tribe or village or wherever you are. That denotes you will hardly meet every requirement that she needs in her life. The first and the most important thing you can do is, have pity and love over her. Talk with her in kind and pleasing sense. And then help or assist her in whichever way appropriate. If it has to give her items then do so. If it has to give her cloth then do so. If it has to give her food then do so. If it has to give her money then do so. If it has to raise her kids

## IMPARTING OF THE MORAL VALUES

then do so. If it has to help her making garden then do so. If it has to help her building house then do so. If it has to give and help her in whatever way then do so. Most of all stay close with her often, and advice or encourage her to live a positive life that is if you are matured enough. Therefore, sharing is caring, and giving is blessing that let your inner personalities outshine.

Orex Kombea

## *GIVING TO THE STRANGER*

Stranger is someone who is alien that is an outsider or a newcomer to your notice in the location or area that where you are. When someone seems strange comes to you, how do you feel and take him/her? Since you know nothing about him/her then what is the first thing that you may do? At first you feel alarmed since both of you are new to each other to know about. But least greet him/her with single word like 'hello'. From there the stranger responds with shy and greeting has to flow before knowing well each of you. (When someone goes to a new place as a stranger he/she is shy but nervous).

You are a stranger going to a new place that everyone and everything there is new to you. How do you feel? What are your emotions like? As a stranger you feel shy and nervous. With that sense of understanding you have to take the stranger in better and positive manner. Approach him/her in an appropriate way sensing that he/she is human being like me. Irrespective of how old he/she

## IMPARTING OF THE MORAL VALUES

is, what race he/she belong, what gender he/she is. Give him/her a positive treatment.

If he/she has to be accommodated then do so in a unique way in whichever way you wish is the best, if he/she has to be appeased then entertain him/her in the way you wish is the best, if he/she to be fed then feed him/her with the food that you wish is the best, if he/she seems poor in cloth then offer him/her with the cloth which you wish is the best, if he/she has to be quenched then provide him/her with drink in whichever way you wish is the best, and do like that in other areas whichever necessary.

Doing the kind actions towards someone who is stranger is the greatest generosity from you, and it becomes the unforgettable lifetime testimony for him/her while being a stranger.

For such concepts in taking the stranger, you can just imagine that if I were a stranger how would I be situated in such approach. In that case you can be a best noble person who can always perform good to the stranger. Therefore, in this cases it becomes the 'sharing is caring', and 'giving is blessing' that is the outshining of the inner personalities.

Orex Kombea

## *GIVING TO THE NEIGHBOR*

When we mean neighbor then it refers to someone who is next to you. Neighbor maybe someone who is your relative or from your tribe. Sometimes neighbor can be someone who is outside from your relative.

Into the urban areas your neighbors are the ones whom are outside from your relatives. Mostly those types of neighborhoods are made from the job colleagues. On the other hand neighbors could be the settlers whom share the common government or company services. Someone who dwells in the house or room bedsides your house or room can be also your neighbor.

Matter of fact neighbor is someone who is very near and rare for your sake. For instance; if you are rarely in desperate need he/she is the first one who will be always there for you. That kind of integrity is always maintained for neighborhood. The tribesmen and the other family members will come for you after him/her. As a human being I value neighbor as someone who is on my side.

## IMPARTING OF THE MORAL VALUES

Hope you as well take neighbor your blooded or immediate relative.

Considering to neighbor is one of the greatest gifts that mankind displays. In that respect how you offer to your neighbor is you know it. Sometimes the neighbor is provided or gifted according his/her needs. Other times the neighbor is invited in the occasions like parties and family gatherings. And he/she has to be informed the necessary and accurate information from you whenever his/her need arise. Also the other essentials that you do for your neighbor when it comes to neighborhood.

What if your neighborhood may not be maintained with love? What if you sometimes offer or make kindness without love inside your heart to your neighbor? What if you offer to your neighbor for the sake of giving or offering? Now, love is one of the most precious and preferable human elements that has to be centered in doing kind or in making offering to the neighbor. In that sense it can become the formal notion that seems the sharing is caring, and the giving idea is blessing that will always outshine your inner personalities.

Orex Kombea

## *GIVING TO THE VISITOR*

You do visit other person. Likewise, other do visit to you. Going to someone is for a reason or a purpose and someone coming to you is for a reason or a purpose becomes the idea of visiting. Giving to visitor means not getting or expecting something from the visitor that whom visits you. But sometimes visitor brings you things like gift, treasure, fortune. Sometimes a visitor is one that brings your food.

How do you take when someone apart from your closeness who comes to you. Take him/her as your visitor. If it means to a visitor then the treatment that you offer to him/her will be different than the normal way you give in your household environments like your family members. The first thing that you offer is greetings and shaking hands or maybe kissing with kindness. After that he/she be welcomed in your environment and comforted whichever way you prefer is the best. And the areas that how you will do to your visitor is the broad way. You do give food and drink, make comfortable bed to sleep, making conversation in kind speeches,

## IMPARTING OF THE MORAL VALUES

avoiding the inconveniences like the children's naughty, not speaking rudely in the house. Above all serve him/her in the special way in the areas that have to treat so that he/she be pleased and feel respected.

If he/she comes to you for expecting things then just simply offer it, that is if you have in place. If he/she visits you in a reason minding that you will provide and give something to him/her then just do so, that is if you have it right. If you do not have them right then just simply say I do not have what you are needed for. Simply say no or give under stable reason to him/her if you do not want to give.

Visitor has to be considered in a kindly approach in your views. Else treat him/her with love and care. What do you feel in your experience whenever you go as a visitor to someone? How do you experience when you be visitor to someone your requirements or needs are not met appropriately? That is when you expect something. Above all treat or take your visitor in the best whichever way appropriates with love and care. From there you will feel the experience of what is visitor mean to you. Therefore,

Orex Kombea

sharing is caring, giving is blessing that let your inner personalities outshine.

# IMPARTING OF THE MORAL VALUES

## *GIVING TO THE ORPHAN*

You must give to the orphan if he/she comes to your approach, because he/she is always in desperate need. The one that misses the treatment from the parents is orphan. The orphan misses both father and mother or one of them. Children become orphan in the minor or kid stage when the parents die. When the orphan child reach to teen stage then it is where he/she is least matured.

While compare orphan with other child whom both of his/her parents are alive. It is a very sad thing. The way of the life of each is different. That means the one that has both his/her parents still alive have the full treatment. The orphan does not. Even the physical look of them is not similar. Apart from all missing treatments that orphan faces is psychologically affected. Sometimes he/she wishes what if my mother/father be alive to parent me. Other times the orphan wishes, what if that handsome man be my biological father when imagining someone, what if that pretty woman be my biological mother when imagining someone.

## Orex Kombea

The situations of the orphan is quite outnumbered which they face in life.

In some places they reason out the situations of the orphans and set orphanages, the institution where orphans are kept. From there most of the orphans are benefited. That means the government or the aid agent is delivering out in love for the orphans. The leaders or the organizing committee has the loving heart. Even the people who work in the orphanage centers are loving ones to orphans. They be credited for such good job.

You as an individual how do you perform for orphan when it comes to your approach? Sometimes an orphan be related to you, sometimes he/she be your neighbor, sometimes he/she be the member of the community that you belong. Not regularly but sometimes the orphan may come to your notice. What if you take ownership and adapt him/her? What if you make him/her become your favorite child? What if he/she be under your custody? What if you make him/her your best friend? What if you be the mentor of him/her? These are few optional suggestions.

## IMPARTING OF THE MORAL VALUES

Well, not every time you are ought to prefer for an orphan. Therefore it is an occasional thing that you are to consider for him/her. Give the best with love and compassion in whichever way you wish. For instance; if he/she has to be clothed then do so with the best way whichever you wish is applicable, if he/she has to be advised then do so with full mentorship, if he/she has to be fed then do so in whichever way he/she be satisfied, if he/she as to be educated then impart with the appropriate standard knowledge. And do well in the other areas that where you wish you can afford for an orphan. In these cases you mostly win the orphan's heart in one way or the other. Therefore, sharing is caring, giving is blessing that let your inner personalities outshine.

Orex Kombea

## *GIVING TO THE WIDOWER*

Mostly pretend to be normal in the life journey of most men whose wives that whom already passed. But some men do not feel normal. They are mostly affected psychologically. They even be physically unbalanced in family wishes. That is maybe they lost their loved partners. They never remarry and live as single till they die. They even be socially unbalanced and live in miserable life. The name widower is given to such men in their wives already passed.

Being widower is different from the others whom their wives are still living with them. The life of widower seems burden in the family wises if his children are minors, or even he has grown-up children. That means the life of raising the children is more challenging, and is a tougher responsibility. Mostly widowers are regarded in that status.

Family life seems balance because both father and mother play the shared roles and responsibilities. The father performs for the both then the life be always tougher and difficult.

# IMPARTING OF THE MORAL VALUES

Simultaneously he becomes both the father and the mother in the family. Sometimes a widower is socially equipped because he is a worker of government, or an employee of a company. That is when the widower life be bit easier. But in some areas most of the widowers are unemployed and poor. Even life seems bit easier for the widowers in the subsisting areas.

Why do you give the widower? When do you share to care? Most of both how do you play yourself for the sake of the widower's case? Response is; whenever it comes to your approach you cannot provide everything that the widower needs, but must share or give the best that you think which will benefit him in one way or the other with love and compassion. For instance; if it has to be given food to him then do so, if it has to be helped him in physical tasks then do so, if it has to be raising his children together then do so, if it has to be making garden or building house for him then do so, if it has to be helped in school fee/tuition fee then do so, do whatever best you wish for him comes your way just do so with love and compassion.

Orex Kombea

To offer effort or kindness for someone like the widower is the great insightful courage and confidence. It is an enforcement and a motivational giving that you as human being to boost the strength of a widower when it comes to your approach. Therefore, sharing is caring, giving is blessing that let your inner personalities outshine.

# IMPARTING OF THE MORAL VALUES

## *GIVING TO THE PARENTS*

Imagine how much do you experience from your mother and father when it means in parenting you. Started from the day one of your life till your present. How much love and care are given by them because of no one but you alone? They feed you, cloth you, carry you, comfort you, wean you, raise you, guard you, guide you, comfort you, educate you, advise you, wash you, nourish you, train you, warm you, support you, concern for you, shelter you. Above of all, especially to your mother who always held your poo and pee to make you clean and healthy every time when you were a baby. Least could father held your pee and poo whenever to make you clean and healthy when you were a baby. Wow! What are great and hero parents they are for your life? They seem the real champions to you. They are real world to you.

Are you going to do anything good in return for your parents? You have an answer for that. But let me reveal few matters of facts being a real child of the parents. Apart from many areas some people do not give back in return to their parents.

Example; if one maybe educated and have decent job, or succeed in life but in return he/she does not do anything worthy and good for the poor diligent parents. Even he/she does not think of paying the debts (school fees/tuition fees) of parents when he/she is employed. Instead thinking of marry or get married and all his/her salary/wage diverts to spouse. This is very miserable and nitwit kind of life which is uncalled for. As a true child of the diligent hero parents you must give first priority in whichever way the best that they always satisfy. Marry before enjoying the life with the parents is morally or socially unsatisfactory. Some parents do not have the heart for such person who does not enjoy his/her success and getting married early.

The subject parents means it is a life to every human being. When giving of doing the things for the sake of parents is area that one has to consider. As you are a son or daughter of your parents just give the best in whatever that you prefer even if you are not biologically related. Or even provide in more or less in their way. If your parents are late then you may take someone who is closed related as your parents. You can even give the best in a sense of

## IMPARTING OF THE MORAL VALUES

parents. If you are married then your father or mother in-law may became your parents since yours are lates. You also share or give them in a best way you think which suits them. Always must share with loving heart in a caring sense. Therefore, concerning to parents is treasured which seems sharing is caring, giving becomes blessing that let your inner personalities outshine.

Orex Kombea

## *GIVING TO THE STUDENT*

Time, money and effort are invested in a particular focal area for the sustainability of the future's living. Student level is the time when certain age group of people especially young whom always spend much for the costs towards their education. Most of the people around you will be students. Even most of your family members or relatives may in the student category. Even yourself maybe a student. Since then every standard or class has the demand to meet.

Mainly government plays the key and the biggest role for students' education. Parents or the family members are the next ones that support in student's education. Finance, cloth and the food are key areas. Sometimes the relatives give hand towards student's education. In other words the help comes as the sponsorship form the charity organizations. Others from the aids like unions into the outside world. There are few more who support in such cases.

## IMPARTING OF THE MORAL VALUES

Some students are not accessible for school fees even though they are willing to go for the smooth flow of learning. There are some factors behind that. They face financial constraints, and social barriers and difficulties. Sometimes a student may face the domestic issues in the family. And other may hails from the family or environment violation. Sometimes a student is orphan. There are more obstacles and barriers that cause hiccups along the journey. Some are vulnerable from the disaster and the social unrest issues.

You will hardly provide or give what you want to give to student in the area where you live. Because there has to be an outnumber in student population. Everyone is always expecting from other people. But you can always make your business to meet the requirements of the student if he/she is your immediate one. It is also a better idea if you want to take the ownership to support a student in your community. It is also a better idea if you contribute towards a student in your area. It is better idea if you provide the basic requirements occasionally for most students in your notice. Least or most you do for anyone seems the giving for the sake of name student. You must do all these kind actions with loving heart and compassion. Therefore, sharing is caring, giving is blessing that let your inner personalities outshine.

# IMPARTING OF THE MORAL VALUES

## *GIVING TO THE COMMUNITY*

It is better you understand your community. It is your pride the community that you dwell in. There is reason being you are a member of your community. You are who you are because of your community. Because of you the community that you live is there. In this sense you know your community well in one way or the other. Hence you know and understand most of its contexts since you are a member of it. They are like the burning issues, the rising or ongoing problems and conflicts, the dialect and language, the needs and wants, the weaknesses and strengths, the achievements, the events, the festivals, the projects, the cultures, the customs, the pride and arrogance, the religion, the government services, the sporting codes, and the others.

There are areas that you as a community member you will perform for it relatively. That is to ensure that being a community member means always player to its stabilities. There are duties and responsibilities that each has to carry out for the community's sake. Perform in duty-bound area is heeded by someone who is delegated for. For example; a councilor brings the government services, a leader who coordinates the activities, a skilled carpenter designs a community synagogue building project, a mechanic fixes and repairs the church or councilor truck, a religious leader who delivers the religious message, a peace officer brings peace, a youth leader coordinates a youth projects, a health worker treats the patients, a women leader organizes women activities, and the others too perform for theirs. These are the people that have the heart for the community. That is where they diligently perform with the best of their ability. Those whom are not dedicated for duty are the participants and the part takers. They also perform to the best of their ability.

If you are the duty-bound then you perform. If you are not a duty-bound but just a member then you perform as well. How do you perform for your community if you a not the duty-bound? As a member you cannot do everything at once and the same time. Even you won't perform in all the areas if you are tasked to perform. But you will perform to a particular area. You won't sit back watching. That is where you love your work. It has to be performed in the

## IMPARTING OF THE MORAL VALUES

best ever way with all your potentials, with all your styles, with all your heart, with all your effort, with all your strength. Above all love your work because you love your community. Therefore, sharing is caring, giving is blessing that let your inner personalities outshine.

Orex Kombea

## *GIVING TO THE ADOPTED CHILD*

Adopted child be someone who has taken by choice into relationship as a son or a daughter of someone. He/She be a sibling of the sons and daughters in a family. Adopted child be sibling to someone who adopts him/her as minor. Adopting a child in his/her minor is reasonable. Adopted father or mother be someone who adopts a child. Adopted child has right to act upon the custody of adopted relatives. Adopted child may adapt to the new environments and new experiences.

There are some reasons or because of some factors people make choice to adopt someone especially the minor one. In most cases a child is adopted because his/her biological parents remarry. The other reason people adopts child is because they are barren or sterile. Next mean of adoption is when a child is orphan. Sometimes a child is adopted because more kids in a single family. Sometimes a child is adopted because he/she is victim especially of the social unrest like the civil war. The other adoptions are sources

## IMPARTING OF THE MORAL VALUES

from the others like the relatives. Also a bachelor and spinster looks for means and ways to adopt a child and they do so.

How do you examine and take your adopted child if it comes to your approach? How do you treat him/her when adopting him/her? Actually some of you have the experience of adopting children. Some of you are currently adopting one or maybe two. Actually it is not an easy experience you adopt a child. The priorities and the treatments are the areas that you will keen on. As a parent or elder sibling you are performing in whichever way you think is the best for a child.

A child has not been neglected and deprived of rights, priorities and privileges. That means feed with care and love, cloth with care and love, has to be educated in proper cause, has not to be discriminated, has not to be stigmatized, has to be housed in a proper sense, verbally not to be abused, as not to be corporally abused, treat in fairness, he/she has not to be teased, as not to be molested, as not be punished in harsh penalty. Instead you must be a good mentor, give good advice, guide him/her well, discipline and counsel him/her wherever error arise, and more others. Last but not the least practice the sense of biological parent with love, care and compassion. Therefore, let sharing becomes caring, and giving becomes blessing that let your inner personalities outshine.

# IMPARTING OF THE MORAL VALUES

## *GIVING TO A PET*

Pet is known be in animal class but some tend to stays with human being. Animal but somehow becomes the companion of human being is incredible. It is an amazing life if an animal class adapt itself to live with human being. No wonder why what really makes them and live together with human being. What makes them be the friend to human being? Pet can be in reptile class, mammal class, bird class, fish class. But mostly birds and mammals are the common ones to stay with human being.

Pets in mammal class are like dog, cat, rabbit, monkey and guinea pig in common. Pets in bird class are like hornbill, cockatoo, cassowary and parrot species especially. In some parts of the world some people take some species of reptile like snake as pet. However, the pets are the wild animals indeed accept most dogs. Because of they are tamed, they be pets. Sometimes they become domesticated. Even some domestic animals become pets. Dolphin in fish class is mostly the tamable one. It is one of the brilliant fishes that performs with gestures in the show with human being as how it has tamed.

Even mostly it is tamed to stay with you as your friend or household member. It is because of you it is there. It may be fleeing from you of fear. It may be not coming to you because you are unrelated to it in animal class. It may be scared because of other pets are already with you. It should have not your close friend because the environment condition is different. But it becomes your friend and stays with you because it has trust and have confidence in you. That is where it lives with you for its lifespan. Wow! What a unbelievable greatest creature?

The pet's right has to be prioritized. That mean never neglect and abuse it. Never do the cruel actions against it. Fit into is shoes. Play with it if it comes in a good sense but never tease it. Feed it with good food that it takes. Make a nice home in friendly environment. Tame it to be friend with other pet if one available. Protect it's offspring if it has one or some. Find its partner if it happens to. Do whatever good and right for it with care, love and

## IMPARTING OF THE MORAL VALUES

compassion. Therefore, sharing tends caring, giving tends blessing that let your inner personalities outshine.

Orex Kombea

## *GIVING TO THE LEADER*

Leader seems someone who takes lead in a particular assigned purpose. Every leader is mandated by people from where he belong to. The name leader, it has to be subjected in various distinguished areas in such like country, province or state, district, society, business, institution, community, organization, religion, group, sport, school and more others. The leadership operations are ranging from the largest to the medium, and from the medium to the small. The contexts of the leadership is far contented. Like for the leadership of the vast areas are more complex and aligned. The context of leadership is far broad and is detail meaning.

Being a leader to carry out his/her assigned duty there are more roles and responsibilities. Some leaders are performing accordingly and effectively. Some leaders are performing ineffectively. The good and the effective honest leader performs according the needs of his/her people. He/She is not self-centered, plays loyally, puts people first and himself/herself last, performs to demote and abort corruption. Bad leader practices corruption,

## IMPARTING OF THE MORAL VALUES

misuses funds, diverts funds for own use, not deliver services to his/her people.

Some leaders are paid. Some leaders work as volunteers. Some leaders are unpaid. Being a leader is not an easy that as expected. Being a leader is pressure and harder. In these cases, how do you as a people of a leader do perform? To be a better person under the leadership of your leader you must submit to your leader, respect your leader, obey your leader, participate in work assigned by your leader, cooperate with your leader, and always perform positively to the standard of your leader's approval. Else, why don't you sometimes provide for him/her like the necessities in money or in food since his/her policy is; 'not a leader first, but the people first'? Or what if you provide him/her with the basic necessities according his/her needs. All your performances have to be with love and care. Therefore, sharing be caring, giving be blessing that let your inner personalities outshine.

Orex Kombea

## *GIVING TO THE SERVANT*

Servant is one who serves another, providing help in some manner. Most servants are paid for what they serve. But some are voluntarily serve. There are distinguished servants which service the different purposes. That means for specifically the servant implements in whatever he/she has to. In terms of name servant, most of them are produced by government. The government employs more people, train them in the specific disciplines, send them over to it's people, and they deliver its services accordingly. The specific areas with their jobs; teacher imparts knowledge to students, police enforce the law and maintain public order, military provides security for country, health worker cares for sick patient, warder keeps inmates or prisoners, and the other specific departments serve in their areas.

Least number of name servants can be found it the specific location. In other words the servants that serve the general public are also known as the servants. For instance; the security guard that serves in a particular premise, a store keeper serves the customers,

## IMPARTING OF THE MORAL VALUES

a banker serves in the bank, a vendor serves customers, a waiter or waitress serves in a hotel, a religious person delivers religious message, a maid or servant serves in Royal Palace, and so on.

You as an ordinary person or maybe one of the servants, do not ever think that everything is always right and better for their operations. As human being he/she faces and goes through some kinds of lives. He/She faces the casualties of challenges. In person he/she is one of your immediate servants. He/She works in your environment because of your sake. He/She works in your community because of your children's sake. He/She works in the area where you live for the sake of your spiritual life.

They have the problems like the financial constraints, they feel sick, hunger and poverty, underpaid, prolonged chronic problems like disease, over deduction, school fee problem, and some more to list. As a servant he/she will not openly emphasize or tell in for the public to aware but instead he/he keeps by himself/her self. Wherefore you as an individual you also give or serve the servant in whichever way you wish is best for him/her with love and compassion. If it has to be fed then you feed him/her. If it has to be sheltered then do so in whichever you wish is best for him/her. If it has to be served in whichever way you wish is best for him/her then do so. Above all, do with love and compassion. Therefore, sharing tends caring, and giving tends blessing that let your inner personalities outshine.

IMPARTING OF THE MORAL VALUES

## *GIVING TO THE FOREIGNER*

Someone is different and strange from your nativeness. Maybe look of him/her is in different race from the race that you belong. The language that he/she uses may different from your dialect. The look of his/her dressing is different from your native. The cultures he/she practice is different from yours. The religious beliefs that he/she has is different from yours. Most of his/her lifestyle is different from yours. That type of person is someone who comes to your country from other country. That person comes from a foreign country and he/she is a foreigner. Sometimes you will take and name him/her an international person.

Because of a reason a foreigner enters your country by law. There are many foreign people that you may notice in your country. Each has his/her own missions or reasons. Foreigner will not come stay with you, or you will not house him/ her unless for genuine reason. Not every foreigner that you notice can not approach your way. But one or two will do. If you are an agent in some areas like foreign affairs or embassies or consular services, and high commission or work in the international trades then you will meet most foreign people. Even you will see most of them in the business operations. The foreign expert academics and scholars in the higher institutions are other lots. In most cases you will see the international tourists.

How will you give to a foreigner? It is not your business you want to give to the foreigner so you will look for him/her everywhere. But once a while you will meet him/her unexpectedly in the times of stranded, mislocate suits, road incident, criminal attack, misfortune, somehow hungry and thirsty, needs your assistance, in difficult situations. You must play your part on that time. Give him/her food and water if he/she is hungry and thirsty. Show him/ her the right location if he/she mislocates. Accommodate him/her if he/she is stranded. Assist him/her if he/she is struggling. Call to police if he/she is attacked or robbed. Call to ambulance if he/she finds road accident. You must show your best colours in those times with love, care and compassion. Therefore, let sharing becomes caring, and giving becomes blessing that let your inner personalities outshine.

# IMPARTING OF THE MORAL VALUES

## *GIVING TO THE DOMESTIC ANIMALS*

Because of you, it is there with you. You are interested in taking care of it. It is not interested in you at first until you agree to look after. Domestic animal is the one that stays close with human being and it tends to be friend or companion of him/her. Mostly the domestic animals are the farm animals. And they are the livestock animals. They are like cattle, horse, sheep, goat, poultry in chicken and duck, turkey, geese, and pig. In the matter of fact those animals can not be kept in the house that you live and look after them like the pet as cat or dog. But they are kept away from human being in some distance measures.

How and when does it sense you in the manner of companion? The first thing first, food. The second thing is shelter. The third thing is yard. The fourth thing is safety. Actually pig and poultry are fed from human hands with intensive care. Cattle, goat, horse and sheep are free ranged and they are placed into a pasture yard. The safety of the animals are paramount to ensure that they are well protected. That means eradicate the dangers like dog, lion, snake and thief. One good experience from the animal to you. They will make all sorts of noises and gestures when they are hungry. That shows that you are their boss and owner. They always expect from you and wait to eat from your hands. They are there because you are the cause. This type of life is practiced in poultry and piggery. It is an awesome lifestyle for a livestock.

Actually most of those animals are not looked after by you. They are looked after by farmer. If you are a farmer, then you know what you do. Else you do not even look after one. But in your look of it, that is how it has to be done. Otherwise it is your experience in looking after one or few. Because of you, it is there with you. Because of you, they are there with you. With that sense, look after them with love and care. Treat them well in good sense. Never apply cruel actions upon them. Feed them on time with right food. Care in appropriate environment. Therefore, sharing becomes caring, and giving becomes blessing that let your inner personalities outshine.

IMPARTING OF THE MORAL VALUES

## *GIVING TO THE HOMELESS*

Homeless is lacking a permanent place of residence. In fact there are some people who have no permanent place to reside. It is not referring to other living thing like animals, but to human being. Do not ever think that every human being has home to reside. There are so many people in some parts of the world who are homeless. That means those types of people live like the nomadic life. This type of case is happening in the developed countries. They move from one location to another looking for the suitable place. In addition to it most of them are also foodless. Wherever they feel that suitable for them to live then they do so. Mostly the residential suits are like the canopy of the town or city shelters, used old cargo containers, debris vehicles, under the bridges, in tents, and in vehicles. On the other sense these kind of people are poor and live the poverty lifestyle. They really live the hopeless life.

In every effect there is a cause. There are so many factors that behind for homelessness. They are like; caused by civil war, from the social unrest like ethnic clashes, the state owns every land that they will make home, no employment or jobless so that they may rent house, their government never concern them into much consideration, no land to cultivate and furrow, less relevant resources to sustain themselves, decline of economic power, higher interpersonal competitiveness, higher tax payments, and more other causing factors.

Just consider him/her if you notice one then. Feel pity on him/her if you notice one lying under the bridge in the night hours. Consider them when you view them live in the tent along the streets. Consider him/her if he/she begs at the streets. Understand him/her if one be filthy. Do not consider him/her inhuman. Offer to him/her if you have sufficient. Advise him/her to live his/her harsh life with positive mind. House him/her if you have sufficient room in your house. Show him/her a piece of land if you have sufficient land. Give/him food or water if you have sufficient. Give him/her money if you have much left from your budget. Do not apply bad behavior towards him/her. After all he/she is a human being like you. Just imagine, how would you be when you were homeless?

## IMPARTING OF THE MORAL VALUES

They really face the life so if you are offering for them, then do with love and compassion. Therefore, sharing tends caring, and giving becomes blessing that let your inner personalities outshine.

Orex Kombea

## *GIVING TO THE JOBLESS*

Jobless people are the ones that not employed or hired according to their skills/knowledge for doing a particular job in a particular area like in a company or a government sector or a private sector. There is someone who is jobless in your community or society that you live. Even jobless people can mean for your whole country. Jobless people can be one person or many in numbers. Jobless people are the ones that have no job to perform. Jobless people are not the ordinary people. They are the skilled people. That means they have been trained for the specific professions. They have some standard of skills, knowledge and experience, however. Sometimes jobless people are the ones who have been experiencing what is working world like for some time back.

The jobless people are the ones that who are looking for job. They do not sit back doing nothing. They move from place to place. They do means and ways to be employed. They write to the management levels or executives for employment opportunities.

## IMPARTING OF THE MORAL VALUES

They even confront the superiors or the top pinnacles in person. However, from the strife and the struggle some are employed, but some are not. Those who are not employed become worse hopeless. They feel exhausted and even sometimes keep up. But they still search for job. So it becomes issue in most of the countries in the world. I may not figure out the root cause of the increases of unemployment rates. And files and files of new graduates heap along the queue to be employed. That becomes the global issue in human resources division.

How do you feel when someone in your family or relative is not employed for so long after achieving better qualification? I am not an employer but I may say that, the ones that are unemployed in your community or society is your concern. Even though you are unrelated culturally. What do you feel if three or four people whom are not employed in a social group of four that you are in? Even yourself may be unemployed. You will not provide a job for them but do some better deeds and show some pathway if it has happened your concern. Assist him/her in the areas like bus fare, accommodate him/her. Give to him/her what he/she needs. Negotiate for him/her about employment to someone who is the boss of a sector or company you know well. Encourage him/her with positive words for success lives. Share your official fashions for job search. Provide him/her with detergent for cleanliness. Feed him sometime with food. Cloth him/her with reasonable decent fashion. Above all do kind things to him/her you wish is best with love and compassion. Therefore, sharing tends caring, giving becomes blessing that let your inner personalities outshine.

# IMPARTING OF THE MORAL VALUES

## *GIVING TO THE ASYLUM SEEKERS*

Someone who is in desperate need to be relieved. Flee from own country to other country due to some harsh causes like the civil unrest or poverty back in their own country or a place that where they live in. This is the most actual factor...... people are seeking for refugee to foreign country out of fear of political persecution or prospect of such persecution in their home country seeking a political asylum. Those types of people are the ones that face the difficult situations along their journey as they travel. You will notice most of the asylum seekers use sea route to travel. They do not follow the proper route rules and regulations. Even sometimes they do not use the suitable or an appreciate transport type. They risk their lives very much along the way. Other type of transport for the them is land as they travel by walk or the other means like train. They move with great fear thinking that they might be meeting dangers along the way. Actually they move with great difficulty. Sometimes they loose lives. But because the difficult situations out there back in the country or place that they live, they keep moving to wherever they aim and wish to live.

They are noticed by the government as they reach their destination country. (They are detected by the human smuggling and trafficking authority.) It is the concern of the government. The government of the country that they reached promptly investigate and interview them. Sometimes they are sent back instantly without considering and concerning. Sometimes they are quarantine for further investigations. Else the government sets detention center according the human rights law amended by the United Nations since the country is part of it.

It is not the job of any ordinary person to deal with and handle such case. Even you will not aware of such case until they put out for notice virally in the public media sources. However, as the concern citizens they make all sorts of both the good and the bad critical comments. Some even really do not like them to settle in. Some even speak verbally the abusive words towards them. Most are complaining a lot. Sometimes those whom are close abuse them physically as they settle. Even most of them conduct

## IMPARTING OF THE MORAL VALUES

protests to government for releasing them out. Some also attempt to attack as well.

We as human being, we will reason out situations first. We will survey them into basic dimensions. It is not your task to detain them. It is not your task to feed them. It not your task to show them the ground. It is not your task to even provide security. It is not your task to maintain their welfares. You just watch what the authority (government) is doing for them. As you are a human being there as to be some manners of contempt, there as to be a reasoning mind, there has to be a compassionate heart, there has to be a caring manner, there has to be a loving sense. What if you were a asylum seeker one time? How would you experience if you were in such situations? You can do good things to them in whichever way you wish is best when they come to your approach in sharing and caring. With the positive understanding sense we must apply a kindness towards such people with love and care. Therefore, sharing tends caring, and giving becomes blessing that let your inner personalities outshine.

Orex Kombea

## *GIVING TO THE SUPERIOR*

In this context we will look at how to give someone in person who is superior. Superior person is someone who is highly ranked. They are superior because they rank much higher than others. They are in the classes as the executives and the decision makers in a particular organization like societies, education institutions, research institutions, firms, business entities, government sectors like education services, religion, financial institutions, and others. You may one of the superiors, or inferior to your superior. They ranked to superior because of their merit. They be in seniority levels because you perform to the juniority levels.

Some of the examples of superiors; the religion leader like pope, denomination head like bishop, business manager, research leader, shopping mall supervisor, school principal, provincial administrator, university chancellor, national sports coordinator, and more on that note. Even you can examine the levels or ranks in your community or society. Your chief or leader is someone the

## IMPARTING OF THE MORAL VALUES

superior. Your ward councilor is someone a superior. A father in a family is someone a superior as well. Someone seems leader in your relatives is known as a superior.

In the basic way of giving to the superior you will look at the structures of services. For that conduct people work from the top down to the bottom levels. In the government or business sectors the employees get paid on their performances. Most of the religious structural jobs are not paid because it not money making institution or profit making organization. As you know, it is just a spiritual work which seems voluntary work.

How do you give to your superior? What do you give your supervisor, and when? Perform to the best of your ability not to please your superior but to meet the standard requirement. Must be up to date in whatever task as assigned for you. Take ownership of what task you are given, and where you are allocated. Be faithful and honest in what you do. Be committed in whatever you do. Sometimes you may identify his/her personal needs and wants that you may provide. Superior does not mean that he/she is always sufficient or have every thing in place for personal use. If you are happened to give then do so. Into religious wises for this idea you are urged to provide most of his/her needs and wants because it is a noble ministry. Always give the best you wish is suitable or appropriate for him/her. Must understand this. He/She is not a super human being. He/He is someone like you in person so give or provide him/her with whatever you wish is best. Because of his/her superity you are working under him/her. With love and kindness you must always give the best to your superior. Therefore, caring tends sharing, and giving becomes blessing that let your inner personalities outshine.

# IMPARTING OF THE MORAL VALUES

## *GIVING TO THE COMMON LAW BREAKERS*

There are some group of people in your society or community who are the common law breakers. In similar sense there are some people who are ethically immoral. This type of person is crime committer, homosexuality, cult worshipper, the bogus cyber scammer or hacker, rapist, murderer, prostitute, gang, child molester, porno star, religious belief backslider, backcross person, marijuana addicted person, drug body, and the others on that note. He/She is convicted because he/she is exposed to the public. He/She is already convicted by moral law. And the people point fingers to him/her saying he/she is a such an immoral person.

Psychologically we put off such person out in our community or area that we live. The concern reason is, they bring shame to the families and community. It seems like they paint the bad image to the community or the area that they live. Sometimes the community's integration has tarnished because its citizens' immoralities. Even their integration has tarnished. They spoil their reputation. They could be penalized by justice system.

## Orex Kombea

As human being there is no one perfect and righteous. Morally or ethically everyone is unrighteous. That means everyone commits immorality. People's immoralities are committed in secret. They are to be committed privately. No body has to notice someone's mistakes. If it is exposed then he/she automatically in the category of the common law breaker. If it is not exposed then he/she continuously doing it and claiming perfect. Irrespective of small or huge immoral behavior. They are still under the immoral activities. That is where every single person in imperfect.

With such understanding do not point finger to someone who is a common law breaker or ethical unrighteous. Instead be contempt, take them as your community member, regard him has your youth. Give guidance and counseling. Advise him/her with brighter words. Show the pathway to the brighter future. Share with him/her that he/she will still have the community trust and opportunities. You can even share with him/her with whatever you wish is best for him/her. If he/she commits immorality for making money the show him/her the other alternative. If he/she a backslider then easily remind him/her pick the older best path.

## IMPARTING OF THE MORAL VALUES

Therefore, sharing tends caring, and giving becomes blessing that let your inner personalities outshine.

Orex Kombea

## *GIVING TO THE CHURCH*

There is an important spiritual workshop which is church. A sick patient visits medical centre or clinic because he/she needs medical treatment. A motor vehicle goes to workshop because it needs repair. A blunted tool get filed to be sharpened. A hunger student has to go to a dining hall to be fed. A thirst has to be quenched. Likewise, your spiritual life has to be perfect and holy before death. It is most important idea when you invest your life in God's kingdom.

You feel relieved in your life when you service yourself by confessing your inequaties. As well as you receive your deliverance and feel blessed when the pastor or servant shares and preaches the godly message to you. You feel good and deliverance when you worship, and sing praises. You feel awe and blessed when you talk to your God that you do not see with your eyes in prayer. It is important in life as to believe some things which you take as your gods. There has to be none other gods than the holiest is your God almighty whom created. The belief system that you

## IMPARTING OF THE MORAL VALUES

have has to be the most focal part of your life, and it has to be granted for your whole living approach.

How do you give to your church? Your pastor is the first priority. Support him in whichever way you wish is best. You must submit under church authority. You must submit under the church board. You must value the church elders and submit under them. You must be kind to other church members. You must participate in every church activity for both the indoor and outdoor. You must contribute and take part in every church project. You must offer to God the blessings from a week. You must pay one tenth to God as your tithe. You must attend to every work soul. Sometimes you must take lead in church activities. All your performances have to be delivered in love and care. In these ways you are giving and serving your church. Therefore, sharing tends caring, and giving becomes blessing that let your inner personalities outshine.

Orex Kombea

## *GIVING TO THE CHILD*

A child is love for father and mother. A child is pride for father and mother. A child is a future for father and mother. A child is a foundation for father and mother. A child seems the world to father and mother. A child is a bridge and the unity for father and mother. A child is a offspring for father and mother. In this chapter father and mother are the major players for the child's sake. If you are other, then can do as you wish but you will not be the full time player in someone's child. But you can perform to the best from your least for the good of a child you give hands. If you are an elder sibling of a child then perform in the best because he/she is your blood.

In this context we will look at the childhood lifestyle which can be protected and guided to wean by father and mother. In a sense of understanding a child by father and mother, it can be weaned child, and even the adult child. But child refers to minor son or daughter. In the childhood from the infancy to puberty, father and mother are in the peak concerning. That means they

## IMPARTING OF THE MORAL VALUES

intensively care for him/her. There are so many things that father and mother do to raise a child. Here are few, they feed and nourish with love, care with concern, cloth with pride and joy, house with security, wash and make healthy, and more.

The other side of the goodness for a child. Feed a child with cognition .... the process of knowing. Father be the good mentor, and mother be the better advisor. First thing; don't let the child notice your (father and mother) privacies, don't let a child override father and mother, don't practice to give money to a child, control the naughtiness of a child, provide the immediate needs of a child like cloth, educate the child with ethical values and moralities, let the child to understand family relationship, educate him/her with the beliefs and the basic religious principles, put him/her in formal learning center like school. Above all give the child's priorities correct. Therefore, sharing tends caring, and giving becomes blessing that let your inner personalities outshine.

Orex Kombea

## *GIVING TO THE DISASTER VICTIMS*

Victims are the ones that affected by some sorts of disasters. Mostly, they are like the war victims, the epidemic victims, the hazard victims. There are some sorts of disasters that pave the way to human being's life. They are to happened in people's lives unexpectedly. That means they are not prepared for it in most cases. They are hit hard. And they are devastated in some measures. They loose many things like properties, surroundings, and relatives or family members. Some may flee from it. They even cost them so much. It takes longer quite some time to relieve and recover. They are in the far extreme and have faced bad situation. More and more lives are lost. They really need assistance and help from the relevant authorities and aid agencies. They are the really victims.

Most of the efforts are burdened by the higher and relevant authorities like the government and the outside aids. In some measures they are recovered but not that fully. Like the widespread epidemic diseases kill more people. The war destroys and kills more people. The disaster like tsunami and earthquake destroy and kill more people. It is terrible when such disasters cost human's lives. Even those relief agencies cannot fix everything in mass. Also human lives cannot be taken back when offered donations and aids.

Those whom survive the disasters are the victims. How and when do you share to care for them. First, feel pity and sorrow on them whenever the news reaches you. Even pray for them. Send condolence messages to them. But most of all you must play the best part in donation. In every disaster, there as to be a donation. That is where you will make donation. Donate the best and good quality. Donate handful rather than handless. Do not donate with penny if you do in money. If one or two of the victims are close to you then just make kindness in whichever way you wish is best for them. If it is to do with food ...then offer to him/her. If it is to do with house .... then accommodate him/her. If it is to do with clothes ... then give him/her the best. Likewise, do the best in other areas. This kind of attitude is completely a sense of love for the victims. Therefore, sharing tends caring, and giving becomes blessing that let your inner personalities outshine.

# IMPARTING OF THE MORAL VALUES

## *GIVING TO THE ELDERLY PEOPLE*

They are the ones that first to see the light of the sun, not you. There are some elder people around you. If it is elder person then it means to someone who is old, greater than another in age or seniority. The people in the elder category are the ones that have created some sorts of experiences or legacies in the community or society. They are the ones that have experience most of the lives. They are the ones that there to face the challenges in life and overcome them. They are the ones that combat the problems and issues of the family or tribe or even community or society where they live. They are the ones that have full of wisdom and knowledge in peace making. They are the ones that are making peace stabilities in a community or a society. Some lots be the ones that contribute immensely in one way or the other for the common goals and ambitions. They may be the experts in a particular areas. They may be the specialists in gifted areas. They are the first ones to see the light of the sun. They are the first ones that experience the stormy weather. They are the first ones that feel the heat of the sun. They have experienced all sorts of lives than you do. And they are still experiencing and performing as you may not. They seem the real people and hero than you.

As an individual person you must take him/her in some measures. Take him/her into some forms of consideration. It is better you value him/her. Respect in some forms of manner. That means submit yourself under him/her by obeying, do not misbehave yourself towards him/her, help or assist him/her if they are happened to, try to be good model like him/her in his/her notice, do not act bully attitudes towards him/her and do teasing noneses.

Since he/she is your elderly person then make him/her pleased or proud by offering or giving the things/essentials according to his/her needs. Feed him/her in mostly in meals if needs arise. Give food and water if he/her is compelled in hunger. Give the decent cloth to him/her according his/her need if you happen to. Give money in whichever amount you wish in sometimes. Do all good what you can do for your elderly person

# IMPARTING OF THE MORAL VALUES

with love and compassion. Therefore, sharing tends caring, and giving becomes blessing that let your inner personalities outshine.

Orex Kombea

## *GIVING TO THE INTERRACIAL*

The scientific knowledge about the human race is very complicated and so detailed in content. But for this context in basic we divide human race in four major groups. They are the Mongoloid race .... the Asian people especially, the Negroid race ... the Black Negroid people especially, the Caucasoid race ... the White people especially, and the Australoid race ... the Aborigine, Melanesian, Veddahs, and Micronesian people especially.

Human being is grouped into races but it is human bound. The colour of the skin and hair are the ones that make the human beings different to each other. Otherwise every feature and every structure is common and similar to each race of people. That means the hemoglobin of the blood is red in pigment for each race. The number of bones present in one's body is equal to every person for each race. All common biological characters like reproduction, excretion, eating, respiration, and others are same to each race. What are the differences among the races? May be the skin color and hair. Otherwise human being is human being.

## IMPARTING OF THE MORAL VALUES

Matter of fact for me, I really love the person who is in not my race. I really do good to them. Even all my social media friends are not the people from my own race in majority but from the other races. That is where I stress, "love is just color blind," Your can love and do good to the people in your own race as well as others. Must be kind to them by doing whatever you wish is best for them. Do not regard them as alien and foreign to you. Love them the most in any dimensions not because of other race but because of mankind. I also really love seeing interracial people marry. It is my wish my future spouse is someone from other race from the race that I belong to. Do not make differences among races and do good to whoever is in other race with love and kindness when he/she comes to your approach. Must be generous and conscious to him/her and be your best in your side because of his/her sake. Therefore, sharing tends caring, and giving becomes blessing that let your inner personalities outshine.

Orex Kombea

## *GIVING TO THE WEALTHY PERSON*

A wealthy person is someone who is rich in resources. He/She has larger amount of money in his/her bank account. He/She has most expensive and valuable items like car or devices. The rich person is someone with many assets. A wealthy person is someone who owns the properties. A wealthy person is someone who invests alot. A wealthy person is someone who is an entrepreneur. A wealthy person is someone who buys many shares. A wealthy person is someone who lives in most expensive homes. A wealthy person is someone who is highly respected. A wealthy person is someone who lives in a luxurious life. A wealthy person is someone who has many business friends. Most of all, a wealthy person is someone who is creative and a hard worker.

Who gives to a wealthy person which is not related to you but member of a community or a society generously? Who gives to a wealthy person without expecting the reward? Wealthy person is someone who is rich with money, and possesses the more valuable items. We always expect in return from the wealthy person when

## IMPARTING OF THE MORAL VALUES

we give any item. We always expect something in return from a wealthy person when we help him/her. We expect anything from a wealthy person when we speak politely. We expect something from a wealthy person when we do kind and good to him/her.

A wealthy person does not need anything from other ordinary person outside of business deals. If it is the case then, won't you give to him/her? But you as good person just kindly present him with very simple but valuable item which he does not have right. Because he has much work load, ask him/her if you can help. Be polite and give much respect to him/her. Offer him with the food which is the ordinary that you eat to him/her. Buy him/her with simple but useful thing that he/she have right not. Do not expect anything from him/her at any time. Give your hands to him/her wherever necessary. Do not feel covet of his/her wealth but have pride in his/her achievement since he/she is your community member. Give him moral support and boost in some ways which are possible. Sometimes you may prepare the best meals for him/her. Do all these deeds and kind actions to the wealthy person with love and compassion. Therefore, sharing tends

Orex Kombea

caring, and giving becomes blessing that let your inner personalities outshine.

# IMPARTING OF THE MORAL VALUES

## *GIVING TO THE LIER AND CON PERSON*

There are so many people who are lazy enough to live a productive, and a meaningful life. That is why many people are living in poverty lifestyle. They are not creative, and hard-working. They always dream a lot. That is why they tell lies and make con talks to convince others of giving them some things valuable like food or money. In the contemporary world there are so many lazy people. They do not know how to work. Even they know how to work but lazy enough. They are creative but not utilizing it. Instead they (even the energetic ones) are depending on other who is hard working. When they are pushed out they move around speaking lying and making con talks to convince other people of giving them something.

In your community or society you are aware and understand some people who tell lies and make con talks to others of giving them something. How are you examining and taking him/her? Actually he/she is not a good person. That is where he/she is put out in people's trust. There is biggest gossip going around everywhere. Even people monitor his/her movements. They even do not want him/her to be invited in the social gathering and feasts. He/She becomes hopeless and eliminated.

This is what you have to do to such person. Do not be rude over him/her. Take him/her as human being. Be calm on him/her and apply kind behaviors towards them. First, in his/her presence do not give the meal you serve. Do not offer to him/her the item that expected for him/her. Even do not accommodate him/her in your home. Rather make an open rebuke to him/her. After all these, apologize to him/her. Then encourage him/her to live hard working and positive life, not the lie and con life, yet meaningful and honest life. Share with him/her one of the useful things like tool that he/can work hard to live. Share something like seed that he/she can plant that will produce food. Share something like animal that he/he can look after or breed. Share the appropriate needs that beneficial so that he/she can sustain a hopeful life by himself/herself. From there he/she will pick up since he/she human being, and again not living the lie and con lives. All what you do for him/her has to be done with love and compassion. Therefore,

## IMPARTING OF THE MORAL VALUES

sharing tends caring, and giving becomes blessing that let your inner personalities outshine.

Orex Kombea

## *GIVING TO THE ENVIRONMENT*

Environment is anything and everything around us. Environment is very important to every life. Likewise it is important for mankind. Environment is diverse and it has the broader knowledge. Geographically environment is comprised of four major elements named the spheres. They are Hydrosphere, Lithosphere, Atmosphere and Biosphere. These spheres play distinguished role and interact to each other so that the whole earth performs its causes.

How and when do we give to environment? There is a saying; you look after environment and it will look after you. The conservation of environment is key concept. According to environment law there are strategies that every mankind has to follow. There are strict laws and regulations to abide in the conserved zones. We use the environments to do all sorts of things to support our lives. We use environment to make food. We use environment to make homes. We use environment to do all sorts of

## IMPARTING OF THE MORAL VALUES

things to support our lives. That is where we care and share for it or give to bless it by conserving it.

Do not be the source and factor to cause any means of pollution in water, air and soil. Do not clear bush and jungle without good reason. Do not cut plants unnecessarily. Stop the cruelness to animal life. Do not set fire in bush or jungle. Do not dump rubbish to sea or running water. Reduce the heaviest smog for the manufacturing industry. Do not dump rubbish in unpermitted area. Care for your environment in the best way you wish. Give to it the best with love and concern. Therefore, sharing tends caring, and giving becomes blessing that let your inner personalities outshine.

Orex Kombea

## *THE SUMMARY*

Give the best to whom you want to rather than optional. Give the best to what you want to rather than optional. We expect in return when we give out things to others .... that type of giving is not good giving. The idea of giving out generously and to forget of returning of giving is magnificent. Caring for others to gain approvals and expecting something in return is not good caring. There are some people who give out to elated or wealthy people and not expecting in return are unique. There are some people who give out without being captured by camera are also tremendous. Care and forget is acceptable morality. Share to someone and expecting in return is not good sharing, but share to forget is good sharing. There are distinguished people whom are to be taken into consideration. They are least advantaged people, wealthy people, elated people, poor people, widower and widow people, orphan people, and others. But it can be given to anybody if you are willing to. In other means, giving does not mean that you will give out or share only items but you can give in kindness. That denotes,

## IMPARTING OF THE MORAL VALUES

give and share with love and compassion by smiling, talk good and polite, respect, greet, assist, humiliation, loyalness, and others.

Sometimes we use to take people into consideration. We give people accordingly irrespective of what status he/she has.

Therefore, sharing tends caring, and giving becomes blessing that let your inner personalities outshine.

Orex Kombea